# 42 All Natural Meal Recipes for Ovarian Cancer:

## Give Your Body the Tools It Needs To Protect and Heal Itself against Cancer

By

**Joe Correa CSN**

## COPYRIGHT

© 2016 Live Stronger Faster Inc.

All rights reserved

Reproduction or translation of any part of this work beyond that permitted by section 107 or 108 of the 1976 United States Copyright Act without the permission of the copyright owner is unlawful.

This publication is designed to provide accurate and authoritative information in regard to the subject matter covered. It is sold with the understanding that neither the author nor the publisher is engaged in rendering medical advice. If medical advice or assistance is needed, consult with a doctor. This book is considered a guide and should not be used in any way detrimental to your health. Consult with a physician before starting this nutritional plan to make sure it's right for you.

## ACKNOWLEDGEMENTS

This book is dedicated to my friends and family that have had mild or serious illnesses so that you may find a solution and make the necessary changes in your life.

# 42 All Natural Meal Recipes for Ovarian Cancer:

## Give Your Body the Tools It Needs To Protect and Heal Itself against Cancer

By

## Joe Correa CSN

# CONTENTS

Copyright

Acknowledgements

About The Author

Introduction

42 All Natural Meal Recipes for Ovarian Cancer: Give Your Body the Tools It Needs To Protect and Heal Itself against Cancer

Additional Titles from This Author

## ABOUT THE AUTHOR

After years of Research, I honestly believe in the positive effects that proper nutrition can have over the body and mind. My knowledge and experience has helped me live healthier throughout the years and which I have shared with family and friends. The more you know about eating and drinking healthier, the sooner you will want to change your life and eating habits.

Nutrition is a key part in the process of being healthy and living longer so get started today. The first step is the most important and the most significant.

## INTRODUCTION

42 All Natural Meal Recipes for Ovarian Cancer: Give Your Body the Tools It Needs To Protect and Heal Itself against Cancer

By Joe Correa CSN

The importance of nutrition can't be overstated in ovarian cancer patients. That's why I want to share this recipe book with as many people as possible who are looking for a natural alternative. The risk of Ovarian Cancer is sometimes higher when you have a family history of cancer in general, being obese or over weight, being post-menopausal, and having an unhealthy lifestyle. Doctors have confirmed that having a well-balanced diet can reduce almost 50% chance of developing most diseases.

Cancer seems to become more and more common in the world due to bad eating habits and stress-filled work environments. Opting for a less intrusive and invasive treatment is always better in the long run as what you eat will eventually affect more than one part of your body.

These recipes will provide you with food combinations that will give your body the most important vitamins in minerals when trying to prevent or fight back against ovarian cancer. The ingredients used will target key sources of anti-cancer compounds that will give your body the resources to bounce back all while eating delicious foods.

Key elements that will help you prevent or recover from ovarian cancer are:

- Vitamins A, B, C, and K
- Crucifers (especially broccoli)
- Omega 3 fatty acids
- Iron and Potasium
- Phytochemicals (plant based nutrients)
- Specific fruits (like sourpop)
- Many others

These recipes are easy to prepare that anyone can make. Enjoy!

# 42 ALL NATURAL MEAL RECIPES FOR OVARIAN CANCER: GIVE YOUR BODY THE TOOLS IT NEEDS TO PROTECT AND HEAL ITSELF AGAINST CANCER

## 1. Bittersweet Mediterranean salad

The high quantity of vitamins A, B, C and K as well as antioxidants in this recipe makes it great to prevent any source of cancer, but we want to stand out the endive's natural characteristics that inhibit ovarian cancer thanks to the Kaempferol found in endives (as in other crucifers), this component can act against the carcinogenic cells in a process called angiogenesis, where the Kaempferol starve off the carcinoma by avoiding the ability of growing blood vessels that feed on them.

**Ingredients:**

1 head Belgian endive

¼ Radicchio

1 Tomato

2 tablespoon Lemon juice

3 tablespoon Orange juice

2 tablespoon Honey

½ teaspoon Turmeric power

1 tablespoon Coconut oil

½ teaspoon Kosher salt

Dash ground black pepper

**Directions:**

1. Wash and rinse all the vegetables;
2. Cut the tomatoes in dices, separate the Radicchio's leaves and cut them in finely slices, slice diagonally the endives into thin strips and mix everything together, add salt and freshly ground pepper;
3. Prepare the vinaigrette by mixing lemon and orange juice, honey, coconut oil, turmeric power and a dash of salt, toss it until well incorporated.
4. Pour the vinaigrette onto the vegetables and enjoy.

## 2. Roasted Salmon coated in fine herbs

The omega-3 fatty acid is well known for helping to protect the heart and brain, but it also seems to restrict the carcinogenic cells from growing, and it's been related to prevent several types of cancers such as: ovarian, colorectal, liver and prostate carcinoma. Likewise, the dill takes action preventing tumors from forming.

**Ingredients:**

1-piece Salmon fillet with skin

2 tablespoons chopped Dill *separate

2 tablespoons chopped Chives *separate

1 Lemon juice

½ teaspoon Kosher salt

Dash Ground black pepper

**Directions:**

1. Preheat the oven to 420°F and prepare a foil-lined baking pan
2. Finely cut the dill and chives into small pieces;

3. Rub the salmon fillet with the herbs, salt and freshly ground pepper, and place it in the pan skin side down.
4. Roast for 10 minutes, add lemon and bake for 3 more minutes.
5. Remove the skin with a metal spatula, serve and sprinkle with fresh herbs.

## 3. Ginger Delight

Ginger and Spinach have amazing properties preventing and attacking carcinogenic cells; Ginger reduces pain and inflammation, stimulates circulation and controls blood pressure. Spinach, on the other hand, has a great amount of chlorophyll which has shown to be effective at blocking the carcinogenic effects of heterocyclic amines which are very destructive to our bodies.

**Ingredients:**

½ Kilo Fresh and washed spinach

1 onion

3 Cm Fresh ginger roots smashed or shredded

1/3 kilo fresh chard

1/3 kilo Zucchini

A pinch or two of salt according to your taste

**Directions:**

1. Boil water and add salt meanwhile cut the onion in 4 pieces and gently put them in the water.

2. Cut the Zucchini in big slices and add them into the water as well.
3. While these are cooked, wash and remove stems from the spinach and chard.
4. When the onions are soft incorporate both the chard and spinach, cover the pot with a lid and let it cook for 7 to 10 minutes.
5. Once the soup is warm but not hot, pour it inside of a blender also add ginger, after that blend everything until getting the desired consistency.
6. Serve it on a plate and Enjoy.

## 4. Soursop Ice-Breaker

In this Recipe I want to emphasize the amazing healing properties of Guanabana or should I say: Soursop; this underrated Caribbean fruit inhibits the urge to be nauseas and vomit, It's also used for sleeping disorders, fevers, and cough but its most important characteristic is that Soursop selectively kills cancer cells unlike traditional chemotherapy which is a very invasive treatment.

**Ingredients:**

1/3 Cup water

1 or ½ cup Soursop pulp or canned juice

2 tbsp liquid yoghurt

1 tspn Linseed

1 tspn almonds and walnuts

A splash of lemon (few drops)

Ice

**Directions:**

1. Incorporate water into a blender, add yoghurt as well.
2. Include Linseed, almonds, walnuts (you can add raisins and any other nuts you like) and lemon drops;
3. Start blending and incorporate ice in multiple batches - not all at once- until you get a very smoothie-like texture.
4. Serve it on a Big Glass.

## 5. Brocolicious Booster

Broccoli as well as every other Crucifer has the potential effect of blocking carcinogenic cells. Broccoli stands out and has proven to be the most effective of crucifers. Scientific studies have demonstrated that it creates a strong defense against lung, prostate, breast, stomach, liver and more importantly, ovarian cancer.

**Ingredients:**

2 medium size broccoli heads

3 cups water

2 cm shredded fresh ginger roots

3 Tbsp sesame seeds

2 garlic teeth

A drizzle olive oil

**Directions:**

1. Chop broccoli in medium size pieces about 2 cm of diameter, cook it by steaming it with water.

2. Add ginger and garlic and mix it with a wooden or plastic spoon. Just one or two times.
3. Incorporate olive oil and let it cook for 15 minutes or until broccoli is tender and soft, don't let it get dry.
4. Meanwhile, heat a pan and toast the sesame seeds a little bit, until they get golden but be careful not to burn them.
5. Once the broccoli is ready, include the sesame seeds mix everything once and serve.

## 6. Zucchini Spaghetti

Zucchini has a high concentration of Iron, Potassium and Vitamin C, but what's interesting is that antioxidants taken from Zucchini can prevent cell mutation which creates cancer, plus it has an incredible flavor and a soft scent when cooking. Also, we'll be using turmeric, olive oil and garlic which are effective preventing carcinogenic cells from growing.

**Ingredients:**

1 Zucchini

250 g Cherry tomatoes

5 garlic teeth

½ spoon turmeric

4 spoons Olive oil

3 leaves basil

**Directions:**

1. Wash the Zucchini and dry it, use the spiralizer to make spaghetti out of it.

2. Pre-heat oven at 356ºF/180ºC, in a deep pan pour olive oil, turmeric and a pinch of salt and pepper, add the tomatoes and mix. Put it in the oven for 30 minutes.
3. In a pan, stir-fry garlic and a drizzle of olive oil.
4. Take the tomatoes out of the oven, mix it with the stir-fried garlic, and add the basil chopped into medium size strips. This mix will be your will be your sauce.
5. Combine both the spaghettis and your sauce and let it macerate for 15 minutes.
6. Serve on a nice plate.

## 7. <u>Veggie Charm</u>

This recipe has all the perks and benefits of vegetables in one meal. It's full of antioxidants, iron and vitamins, but what is really important, is that it has plenty of "Phytochemicals" which are plant based nutrients known for their effectiveness decreasing ovarian and prostate cancer risk.

**Ingredients:**

½ a carrot cut into ¼-inch-thick stripes

1 Eggplant, cut into ¼-inch-thick stripes

1 Zucchini cut into ¼-inch-thick stripes

½ bell pepper cut into ¼-inch-thick stripes

200 g mushrooms cut into thin slices

100 g cabbage cut into small stripes

4 teeth of garlic

Olive oil

salt

**Directions:**

1. In a wok or a deep pan, sauté the carrots with a drizzle of olive oil and garlic.
2. When the carrots get tender, incorporate the eggplant, zucchini, bell pepper, the cabbage and the mushrooms, moisturize with a drizzle of olive oil, and stir occasionally.
3. Cook it for 20 minutes or until everything is tender and gold-ish colored.
4. Serve in a plate and pair it with 2 or 3 slices of toasted bread.

## 8. Whole wheat banana-nutty bread

The benefits of ripe bananas have been associated with anti-carcinogenic properties, as the bananas ripens they produce a substance called Tumor Necrosis Factor that kills the carcinogenic cell that will definitely help prevent you from growing any tumors. They also provide a large amount of high quantity vitamins and fiber that will improve your digestion.

**Ingredients:**

4 tablespoons Coconut oil

1/3 cup Honey

2 eggs

1 cup mashed well-ripe bananas

¼ cup Greek yoghurt

1 teaspoon vanilla extract

½ teaspoon cinnamon

1 teaspoon baking powder

½ teaspoon baking soda

1 ½ cup whole wheat flour

½ cup chopped walnuts

**Directions:**

1. Preheat the oven to 350° F. Slightly grease a loaf pan.
2. Mix together the coconut and honey until well combined, add the bananas, yoghurt, vanilla, cinnamon, baking powder and baking soda.
3. Beat the eggs and add them into the mixture.
4. Incorporate the flour in batches, stirring gently while adding the walnuts. The mixture doesn't have to be homogenic.
5. Pour the batter into the prepared pan and bake for about 40 minutes or until browned and inserted toothpick come out clean.
6. Allow the bread to cool for a few minutes, transfer it to a rack and let it cool completely before cutting.
7. Pare it with PB and Jam.

## 9. Morning Boost Essential

Preventing cancer is all about creating healthy food habits, and nothing cleans your body as good as a revitalizing morning tea. Green tea, lemon, blueberries and bananas provide lots of vitamins and antioxidants. Turmeric adds an essential component to this morning boost, its miraculous spices provide powerful benefits to our health including preventing ovarian and other types of cancer.

**Ingredients:**

1 teaspoon Green tea leaves

½ teaspoon Turmeric

1 cup hot water

1 Lemon juice

Honey to taste

½ cup Blueberries

1 Banana

½ cup quick-cooking Oatmeal

1 ½ cup Milk

Dash Cinnamon

Dash of salt

**Directions:**

*For the tea

1. Pour the tea leaves into hot water, add the Turmeric and set aside for a few minutes;
2. Add the lemon juice and honey to taste;
3. Serve warm.

*For the oatmeal

1. Heat the milk in a medium saucepan;
2. When it starts to simmer add the oatmeal and let it boil;
3. Lower the heat and stir until reaching the desire consistency;
4. Remove from the heat and add the fruits, cinnamon and salt;
5. Add honey to taste and serve warm.

## 10. Refreshingly Fruit Salad

Getting all the vitamins your body needs is essential to preventing any kind of illness. Understanding that nutrition is the foundation for a healthy life is the first step. This Refreshingly Fruit Salad aims to calm all your cravings for sweets while providing vitamins, antioxidants and fibers.

**Ingredients:**

1 Red Apple

2 Kiwis

5 ounces Dates

¼ cup Brazil nuts

½ cup Greek yogurt

Honey to taste

**Directions:**

1. Wash and cut the apple in cubes;
2. Cut the kiwis in half and scoop them with a soup spoon, cut them in cubes;
3. In a bowl pour the apples, kiwis and dates;

4. Add yoghurt and mix together;

5. Add honey to taste and enjoy.

## 11. Spicy Shredded Salad

This spicy salad is made with two essential ingredients that contribute to preventing all sorts of cancers. We're talking about carrots and cabbage, the *falcarinol* in the carrots, and the *glucosinolates* found in cabbage are both effective against cancer, because they inhibit the uncontrolled cell growth characteristic in the cancer mutation process.

**Ingredients:**

2 cups Water

3 tbsp apple Vinegar

1 Carrot

¼ Cabbage

1 Chili Peppers

2 tbps Olive oil

2 tbps Honey

2 tbps Dijon Mustard

1 Lemon juice

½ tsp Salt

Fresh Ground Black Pepper to taste

**Directions:**

1. In a saucepan boil the water;
2. Meanwhile shred the carrots and cut the cabbage and chili peppers in thin stripes;
3. When the water starts to boil add the salt and vinegar;
4. Low the heat and add the vegetables until the water simmers and remove from heat;
5. In a bowl prepare the vinaigrette mixing the olive oil, honey, mustard, lemon, salt and pepper until well combined;
6. Rinse the vegetables and pour the vinaigrette onto them, toss to incorporate and enjoy.

## 12. Bee Pollen-Cocoa Bars

If you are into sweets but want to take care of your health, you have to try these bee pollen-cocoa bars. Delight yourself with the perks of cocoa and bee pollen. Cocoa has up to three times more antioxidant flavonoids than green tea, also the polyphenols found in this plant have shown to stop and reduce the proliferation of breast, prostate, colon, and ovarian cancer. In the other hand, bee pollen provides a great source of vitamins, minerals, good carbohydrates, and protein for our bodies.

**Ingredients:**

1 Teaspoon Bee Pollen

½ cup cocoa powder

2 cup walnuts

1 cup almonds

½ dark chocolate chips

2 cups dates

¼ teaspoon of Salt

**Directions:**

1. Chopped the almonds and set aside;
2. In a food processor combine walnuts, cocoa, bee pollen and salt to form a fine powder;
3. Add clean dates, one at a time, combining until form a crumbly mix;
4. Transfer to a bowl and incorporate chopped almonds, folding the almonds into the mixture;
5. Use a 9x9" silicone pan to spread the mixture, sprinkle with chocolate chips and gently press them down;
6. Refrigerate up to 1 or 2 hours before cutting them into bars.

## 13. Cranberry-Poached Apples

Organical cranberries are rich in *Perillyl Alcohol*, which are related to destroying a variety of carcinogenic cells. While green tea aids to promote weight loss, been overweight is one of the most common problems related to ovarian cancer development, it also has many other attributes such as protecting cells from DNA damage caused by free radicals, playing a key role against cell metastasis.

**Ingredients:**

2 to 3 Apples

2 cups Water

4 Tbsp Honey

1 Orange zest

1 Lemon zest

1 Lemon juice

1 Cinnamon stick

1 Cardamom pod, grounded

1 Vanilla bean

1 tea-bag Green tea

1 ½ cups Cranberries

**Directions:**

1. In a saucepan with water put the apples, honey, orange zest, lemon zest, lemon juice, cinnamon stick, ground cardamom and vanilla bean, bring to boil, then reduce heat and simmer for about 15 minutes;
2. Add green tea and cranberries and stir all the ingredients, return to a simmer for 3 more minutes;
3. Transfer to a heat-proof bowl and let it cool;
4. Discard lemon and orange zest, cinnamon stick, vanilla pod and tea bag;
5. Refrigerate overnight and enjoy.

## 14. Lentil and Flax Soup

Flaxseed or Linseed is an incredible source of fiber, omega 3 fatty acids and lignin. This component has been shown to reduce carcinogenic tumors, and are commonly used in treatments for breast, prostate, and ovarian cancer. Celery, onion, carrots, and tomatoes also enrich this recipe providing more perks in your daily plan for cancer prevention.

1 Carrot

2 Celery sticks

1 Onion

1 Green Pepper

2 Garlic gloves

4 cups Boiling Water

2 cups Chicken broth (preferably homemade)

4 Peel tomatoes

Dried bay leaf

1 ½ cups Dried lentils

½ cup Ground Flaxseed

1 tablespoons flaxseed oil

1 to 2 tsp Salt

Fresh Ground black pepper to taste

½ tsp Chili powder

½ tsp Turmeric powder

**Directions:**

1. Cut the carrots, celery, onion, green pepper and garlic into pieces;
2. In a pan with flaxseed oil sauté carrots, celery, onions, green pepper and garlic stirring occasionally for about 15 minutes;
3. Meanwhile, boil some water and cooked the tomatoes for five minutes, remove from heat and add cold water whilst peeling the tomatoes, reserve for later;
4. When the carrot and peppers are tender, add boiling water, chicken broth, peeled tomatoes, lentils, salt,

ground pepper, chili powder and turmeric powder, stir and let it boil, low the heat and let it simmer for 1 hour or until the lentils are soft;

5. Add the ground flaxseeds, let it rest for five minutes and serve.

## 15. Healthy Greek Salad

When it comes to preventing cancer, the best you can do is go green with your food. In this recipe you can enjoy the benefits of dill, tomatoes and cucumber, which thanks to their components and properties have the ability to prevent and fight ovarian, breast, uterine, and prostate cancers.

**Ingredients:**

2 tbsp Red-wine vinegar

3 tbsp Extra-Virgin Olive oil

1 tbsp Fresh dill, finely cut

Half Romaine lettuce

2 Tomatoes

1 Cucumber

½ Red Onion

½ cup Greek Yoghurt

1 tsp Salt

Fresh Ground pepper to taste

**Directions:**

1. Chopped the tomatoes and cucumber in squares, cut the romaine lettuce and onion into stripes;
2. Add salt, olive oil, vinegar, ground pepper and yoghurt;
3. Mix everything together, serve and sprinkle with fresh dill.

## 16. Mango Passion Dessert

Mango is an appetizing and mouth-watering fruit that has several compounds that have been linked to anti-cancer and anti-inflammatory activities; these compounds include Vitamin C and Beta-Carotene.

**Ingredients:**

2 ½ to 3 Cups of Chilled yoghurt / curd.

2-3 medium-size mangoes, chopped *I used alphonso mangoes.

1 cup almonds or walnuts *optional.

¼ Tsp saffron *optional; it will color your dessert. Sugar as much as you need or want *you could use honey or brown sugar.

You may use Chopped mangoes as a garnish.

**Directions:**

1. Mix the yoghurt or curd with the sugar until smooth.
2. Pour in the mangoes and saffron as well as the nuts.
3. Mix very well

4. Serve it in any cup you may like and pair it with some chopped mangoes.

## 17. **Tomato Pie**

Tomatoes have an enormous amount of Lycopene, which reduces the incidence of cancer diseases, especially ovarian, prostate, and lung cancer. That's why I decided to use tomatoes and olive oil in this recipe to extract all the benefits and enjoy them in the form of a pizza.

**Ingredients:**

1 whole wheat pie crust

1 tomato cut in medium size slices

a drizzle of olive oil

salt and pepper to taste

Directions

1. Pre-heat the oven at 250ºF.
2. Cover the surface of your crust pie with your sliced tomatoes.
3. Pour olive oil all over the tomatoes, sprinkle salt and oregano too.

4. Put it in the oven, until tomatoes get a little bit dry and the crust is golden.

## 18. Shiny Mushroom

Ancient Egyptians believed that eating mushrooms brought long life, and they weren't too wrong after all, many studies have shown that mushrooms contain a substance called Lentinant which can help increase the survival rate of cancer patients.

**Ingredients:**

½ kilo of mushrooms (champs).

200ml of White Wine.

Pepper and salt to taste.

Olive oil.

**Directions:**

1. Clean and slice the champs.
2. Start heating a pan until it gets very hot, then incorporate the mushrooms with a little bit of salt. Don't use Olive oil yet.
3. Put a lit to the pan, and let it cook in medium heat for a while, until they start running out of their own water.

4. Pour the Cava in and stir it a bit and let it reduce, add a dash of pepper and a bit of water.
5. Keep pouring water until champs get tender then stop, when all the water is evaporated drizzle them with olive oil and let them rest for 5 minutes.

## 19. Green Cream

In this exquisite and mouth-watering recipe, we want to highlight the benefits of asparagus. This green and leafy vegetable has some powerful reasons to be part of your nutritional life. It has an effective way to eradicate Oxidative Stress from our bodies which reduces the possibility to destroy benign cells.

**Ingredients:**

250-300 g Asparagus

100 g Green Peas

1 Lt Water or Vegetable Broth

1 Red Apple Chopped into little pieces

2 Tbsp Olive Oil Extra-Virgin

200ml Almond Milk

1 Tbsp Ground Flax Seeds

salt to taste

**Directions:**

1. In a saucepan boil all the water and milk; while the water boils, wash the asparagus and remove the hardened part and discard them, chop the asparagus into little pieces and keep the Head aside.
2. Gently add the asparagus into the water and let it cook for 15 minutes.
3. Wait until everything is a bit warm, add the apple and a drizzle of olive oil.
4. In a skillet or pan, heat the oil and sauté the asparagus tips for a few minutes.
5. With a blender, mix everything in different batches; be careful not to do it all at once.
6. Serve your plate with the asparagus tips like Garnish.

## 20. Banana Mix Breakfast

In this amazing recipe not only will you find a tasty and interesting way of eating grains and seeds, but you will also be able to enjoy the benefits of a substance called TNF that has the ability to combat abnormal cells and enhance immunity against cancer.

**Ingredients:**

1 cup ground flax

1 Tbsp coconut oil

1 ½ Banana *blueberries, walnuts, raisins are optional.

Sprinkle salt

Sprinkle cinnamon

**Directions:**

1. Mix all the ingredients in a food processor
2. Make little patties
3. And they are ready to eat; you can warm them up in a pan.

## 21. Tropic-Asian Soup

This tasty and spicy soup is all you need to boost your day. Get the advantages of ginger, jalapeños, mushrooms, pineapples, tomatoes, and more all in one delicious soup. From the outstanding anti-inflammatory properties of ginger to the selenium and beta-glucans found in shiitake mushrooms. All the ingredients in this recipe will help you to prevent and fight ovarian cancer.

**Ingredients:**

1 tbsp Lemongrass

1 tbsp Ginger, grated

3 cups Chicken broth

1 Jalapeño

200 gr Chopped fresh pineapple

200g Shiitake Mushroom

300 gr Shrimps

2 Tomatoes

1 Red bell pepper

1 tbps Fish Sauce

1 Lime Juice

Scallions

Coriander

**Directions:**

1. Smash ginger and lemongrass until resembles to a paste;
2. In a saucepan bring broth and jalapeños to boil and add the ginger paste, low the heat and let it simmer for 15 minutes;
3. Meanwhile, cut pineapples, mushrooms, tomatoes and bell peppers into cubes;
4. Remove the solids from the chicken broth and add the vegetables and pineapples in cubes, fish and eel sauce, simmer for 5 more minutes;
5. Add the shrimps and let the cook for 3 minutes;
6. Remove from heat and pour in the lemon juice, scallions and coriander finely chopped;

7. Serve hot and enjoy.

## 22. Grilled Chicken Skewers

Grilled skewers are a fun way of eating healthy. They're very versatile allowing you to play with flavors and ingredients all while taking care of your health. You will benefit from components such as *bromelain* found in pineapples, which has an antitumoral effect superior than the chemo drug 5-fluorauracil used in regular cancer therapy, the *allicin* in garlic that reduces the risk of developing cancer, and many others.

**Ingredients:**

2 Chicken breasts, diced

2 Lemon Juice

1 tbsp Fresh Rosemary

1 tbsp Fresh Oregano

2 Garlic gloves, minced

Fresh Ground black pepper to taste

1 tspn Salt

250 gr Pineapple

250 gr Red and green bell pepper

100 gr Red onion

**Directions:**

1. Finely chop rosemary and oregano;
2. Mix lemon juice, garlic, ground pepper, rosemary and oregano;
3. Pour this mixture into the chicken breast and let it marinate for one or two hours;
4. Prepare you grill;
5. Cut the pineapples, bell peppers and onions into squares;
6. Remove the chicken from the marinade and thread it onto the skewers alternating with onion, pineapple and bell pepper pieces;
7. Pour some of the remaining marinade over the skewers and start to grill;
8. Grill for 15 minutes covering the skewers with the marinade to maintain the moisture.

## 23. Fruity Healing Salad Sensation

This fruity salad not only has an incredible taste, but also provides a high amount of nutrients and compounds needed in the prevention of cancer. Such is the case of the *ellagic acid* found in raspberries, which is capable of killing cancer cells (apoptosis) and is a natural anti-carcinogenic and anti-mutagen; in addition, the *garcinone* in mangosteen contribute towards the goal of preventing and fighting cancer.

**Ingredients:**

1 ½ cup Raspberries

1 Mangosteen, peeled

Half Avocado

¼ cup Almonds

Half Romaine lettuce

Half Radicchio

2 tbsp Red-wine vinegar

3 tbsp Extra-virgin olive oil

½ tsp Salt

Fresh ground black pepper to taste

**Directions:**

1. Put half cup of raspberries, oil, vinegar, salt and pepper into a blender to make the vinaigrette;
2. Dice the mango and avocado, chop the almonds, and cut into stripes the lettuce and radicchio, mix everything together and sprinkle with a dash of salt and pepper;
3. Pour the vinaigrette onto the salad, toss gently, serve and enjoy.

## 24. Fruity Ice-cream yoghurt Surprise

Eating well can also mean eating delicious and healthy food. That is what this ice-cream yoghurt is all about. Taking advantage of the benefits of pineapples and mangos, due to the presence of *bromelain* in pineapples and *beta-carotene* in mangoes, this recipe focuses on preventing most diseases.

**Ingredients:**

2 cups Mango, peeled and diced

2 cups Pineapple, peeled and diced

3 leaves Mint

1 Cardamom pod

Honey to taste

1 ½ cups Greek Yoghurt

**Directions:**

1. Cut the mango and pineapple into cubes and freeze them overnight;

2. In a blender put the yoghurt, honey and cardamom, start to blend;
3. While blending, gradually toss the frozen pieces of mango and pineapple until reach a creamy texture;
4. Add mint leaf on top and enjoy immediately.

## 25. Cold Cucumber Soup

Did you know cucumbers can also be eaten cooked? Somehow, they turn into sweet bites perfect to ensemble a creamy and delightful soup. They are also wonderful for our health, aiding towards the fight against ovarian, breast, uterine, and prostate cancer because of its lignans that have been shown to reduce the risk of tumor growth.

1 garlic glove, minced

1 Lemon Juice

1 Cucumber

4 cups Vegetable broth

1 teaspoon Salt

Fresh ground pepper to taste

1 Avocado

1 cup Greek Yoghurt

60 gr Almonds, chopped

**Directions:**

1. Sauté the minced garlic in a saucepan with oil;
2. Add lemon juice and stir;
3. Add the cucumber in dices, broth, salt and pepper, simmer for 5 minutes and let it cold;
4. Transfer to a blender, incorporate avocado and blend everything together;
5. Refrigerate until chill;
6. Chop the almonds;
7. Serve it cold with a couple of spoon of yoghurt and sprinkle with chopped almonds.

## 26. Broccoli Sprout Booster

We all have heard about how good broccoli sprouts are at neutralizing cancer cells from growing and the unbelievable amount of antioxidants it has, but also broccoli sprouts contain *sulforaphane* which boost up your body's production of cancer protective enzymes, these enzymes can also kill *Helicobacter pylori,* ulcer-causing bacteria linked to stomach cancer.

**Ingredients:**

¼ fresh grapefruit juice

2 Tbsp All-fruit blackberry preserves

2 Tbsp Flaxseed oil

1 Tbsp Extra-Virgin Olive Oil

Salt and pepper to taste

120 g Broccoli Sprout

6 cups arugula

1 cup mango cut into cubes

½ cup chopped almonds

1 cup blackberries fresh or frozen.

3 fat-free cheese medium size balls

**Directions:**

1. In a small bowl mix together grapefruit juice, blackberry preserves, olive oil and flaxseed oil, whisk well until the mix is slightly hardened. Season with salt and pepper to taste, and set aside; this mix will be the dressing to the salad.
2. In a large bowl add broccoli sprouts, arugula, mangoes, almonds and cheese.
3. Pour the dressing into the large bowl until the sprouts and arugula are lightly coated; stir together a couple of times and refrigerate remaining dressing.
4. Serve and garnish with the cheese balls and blackberries.

## 27. **Fruity Cereal**

Oats have an incredible ability. When you soak them they allow enzymes to break down and neutralize phytic acid, a compound that can block the absorption of many minerals. Buckwheat has a large number of health benefits like the reduction of blood pressure, improving our digestive system but most importantly they are a great source of antioxidants which eliminate carcinogenic cells.

**Ingredients:**

1 ½ rolled oats

½ cup puffed organic buckwheat

½ cup dried apples, chopped

2 tsp ground cinnamon

1 cup grapes, halved

3 Tbsp brown sugar

Rice Milk

Enough water to soak oats

**Directions:**

1. Pre-heat oven at 325ºF.
2. Spread the oats evenly over a non-stick baking tray and toast them inside of the pre-heated oven for 10 minutes, mix and stir every now and then, pay extremely attention when toasting because oats tend to burn fast.
3. Remove the oats from the oven and let it cool, pour them into a large crystal bowl and soaked them in water and leave them overnight.
4. The next day, add the buckwheat, dried apples, cinnamon and brown sugar to the soaked oats. Mix well.
5. Pour the mixture in a ceramic bowl and serve it using pears and grapes as garnish and pair it with rice milk.

## 28. **Fit Breakfast Muffins**

Carrots are very famous due of their ability to provide beautiful skin or enhance our eye sight. It also contains Falcarinol which is a very strong and natural anti-cancer chemical.

**Ingredients:**

1 ½ cups whole-wheat pastry flour

¼ cup wheat germ

¼ cup ground flaxseed (preferably golden)

1 ½ tsp baking powder

1 tsp ground cinnamon

2 eggs, beaten

2 tsp vanilla extract

2 finely grated and peeled carrots

¼ cup grounded nutmeg

¼ tsp salt

¾ cup low-fat milk

1/3 maple syrup

1/3 cup brown sugar

½ cup raisins

¾ chopped toasted walnuts

**Directions:**

1. Preheat oven to 350ºF, cover the muffing cup with olive oil.
2. Stir together, whole wheat, wheat germ, ground flaxseed, baking powder, ground cinnamon, ground nutmeg and salt.
3. Put milk, syrup, brown sugar, eggs and vanilla until all the sugar dissolves. Softly stir in carrots, raisins and walnuts.
4. Divide equally among the molds or the muffin cups and bake for 20 to 25 minutes or until you insert a toothpick in the middle of one of the muffins and it comes out completely clean.

## 29. Golden Quinoa

It's a little bit sweet and a little bit salty. You will find a perfect mix in this recipe. Quinoa is a great source of soluble Fiber, spinach provides all the beta-carotene and vitamin C needed and ginger, turmeric and cherries, all contain antioxidant and anti-inflammatory properties. Everything you need in one food.

**Ingredients:**

2 Tbsp coconut oil

1 1-inch piece fresh ginger (peeled and grated)

1 Tsp ground turmeric

¼ Tsp ground cumin

1 Tsp ground coriander

1 cup golden quinoa (well washed and drained)

1 ½ cups water

¼ cup dried tart cherries (chopped) *Optional

1 cup chopped spinach

½ bell pepper cut in thin slices.

1/2 cup thinly sliced green onions

1/4 cup fresh lime juice

**Directions:**

1. Simmer in a medium pot, coconut oil with ginger, turmeric, cumin and coriander until fragrant
2. Incorporate the Quinoa with the bell pepper and stir well, after that add water and let it boil, as soon as it boils reduce the heat, cover it with a lid and let it simmer for 15 minutes or until all the water is absorbed.
3. Pour in lime juice and add the green onions, spinach and cherries. Season to taste with salt and pepper. Serve and enjoy

## 30. <u>Red Power</u>

In this recipe you will find an incredible amount of antioxidants and Lycopene, which are responsible for preventing ovarian cancer. You will also feel the benefits of basil leaves, which increase antioxidant consumption and healthy enzymatic activity.

**Ingredients:**

(400g) tins chopped tomatoes

400ml chicken or vegetable stock

1 Tbsp sugar

15 leaves fresh basil

2 Tbsp olive oil

250ml Whole milk

**Directions:**

1. Simmer both the tomatoes and the stock. Cook for 10 minutes

2. Incorporate sugar and basil. Add sugar to taste
3. Add Milk slowly and oil stir and cook for another 10 minutes
4. Serve with a few leaves of fresh basil as Garnish

## 31. **Coconut Fish**

For this recipe, we are using a group of important ingredients which are: ginger, onion, and garlic, which provide anti-carcinogenic, anti-fungal, anti-bacterial and anti-inflammatory properties.

**Ingredients:**

1 fillet preferred White fish

2 Garlic gloves

1 Red onion

1 tbsp Ginger

400 ml Coconut milk

¼ cup Corn

1 tbsp Thyme

1 tsp Kosher Salt

Fresh Ground Pepper to taste

**Directions:**

1. Preheat broiler to high heat and line a baking pan;

2. Smash the garlic and kosher salt forming paste, add oil, thyme and pepper;
3. Place the fish in the pan, spread the paste onto the fish a set aside;
4. In a saucepan sauté the garlic, onions, corn, and ginger until almost cooked;
5. Add the coconut milk while stirring and let it simmer for 7 minutes stirring occasionally, check salt and pepper;
6. Meantime, put the fish in the broiler and cook for 7 minutes;
7. Serve together and enjoy.

## 32. Delicious Sticks

Fully charge your anti-cancer diet by eating asparagus. As we said before asparagus is a vegetable well packed with beta-carotene, glutathione, vitamin C, and N-acetylcysteine; plus, this delectable recipe contains walnuts which are rich in anti-mutagen and anti-carcinogen vitamins, nutrients and natural Phytochemicals.

**Ingredients:**

500 g asparagus spears washed and trimmed

2 tsp fresh ginger, grated

2 tbsp quince jam

2 tbsp Extra-Virgin olive oil

1 tsp lemon juice

3 tbsp walnuts, chopped

Salt and pepper to taste

**Directions:**

1. Prepare a steamer with boiling water, put the asparagus in and cover it with a lid; steam for 3 to 5 minutes or until tender crisp.
2. Transfer hot asparagus to a serving plate.
3. In a small bowl mix together ginger, quince jam, olive oil, lemon juice, salt and pepper.
4. Pour the mixture over the asparagus and sprinkle with walnuts.

## 33. Nettle Pesto

It might sound crazy to add Nettles to this recipe but it will do your body good. Young and blanched nettles are 100% edible and contain a whole lot of antioxidants and flavanoids. The pasta in this recipe is a very healthy alternative to regular pasta.

**Ingredients:**

1 cup young nettle leaves, blanched.

4 garlic gloves peeled

2 Tbsp walnuts, chopped

3 Tbsp parmesan cheese, grated

Enough extra-virgin olive oil as you may need

170 g dried whole-wheat pasta

**Directions:**

1. Process nettle leaves, garlic, and walnuts with a food processor. Process it while gently and gradually adding olive oil, until getting the desired consistency.
2. Add the cheese into the mixture and stir well.

3. Cook pasta according to the package instructions.
4. Drain pasta and put it back into the pot.
5. Stir in the nettle pesto; mix well, and serve on serving plates.

## 34. **Barley and Beans**

Diets based on Beans are being directly associated with a high risk reduction of several types of cancers being ovarian cancer at the top of that list. The tomatoes and basil added in this recipe have a long list of anti-cancer properties as they both have antioxidant agents.

**Ingredients:**

1 onion, chopped

1 small carrot, peeled and diced

½ rib celery, finely chopped

1 tbsp Extra-Virgin oil

3 cups vegetable oil

¼ cup pearled barley, cooked

¼ cup white beans, cooked

¼ cup canned tomatoes

2 or 3 garlic gloves *to taste

2 Tbsp of fresh basil, chopped

½ tsp dried rosemary

Salt and pepper to taste

**Directions:**

1. In a soup pot sauté in olive oil the onions, medium heat for 5 minutes or until tender and shiny.
2. Add celery and carrots; simmer for 4 minutes.
3. Pour in gently the vegetable broth and bring it to a boil, let the soup simmer until carrots and celery are tender.
4. Incorporate to the mixture the barley, canned tomatoes, garlic, rosemary and basil, simmer it for a few more minutes.
5. Season it with salt and pepper, serve on deep plates and enjoy.

## 35. Horseradish Tunas Steaks

For this plate we are focusing on the benefits of turmeric and horseradish. The first one is an Indian spice, used for its medical benefits. Research indicates that turmeric can treat a wide range of illnesses, but in the case of cancer it can act by identifying potential carcinogenic cells and induce apoptosis. On the other hand, it also has compounds that suppress the growth of tumors.

**Ingredients:**

2 Tuna Steaks

1 cup Almond flour

1 cup Breadcrumbs

1 tsp Turmeric

1 Egg

1 tbsp Horseradish, grounded

1 tbsp Ginger, minced

3 tbsp Olive oil

1 Lemon Juice

1 tsp Salt

Fresh ground pepper to taste

**Directions:**

1. Rub the tuna with salt and pepper;
2. In a large bowl, mix together, almond flour, breadcrumbs, minced horseradish and garlic;
3. Put the egg in another bowl and slightly beat it;
4. Pass the tuna steaks through the egg and the coat them with the almond flour mixture;
5. Heat a skillet and coat it with olive oil;
6. Fry the steak until golden brown for both sides;
7. Add lemon and serve with your favorite salad.

## 36. **Wild Cookies**

Another astonishing ingredient that's included in this list are rose hips. These are the fruits of rose plants and they're packed with anti-carcinogenic properties largely due to the richness in *proanthocyanidins, phytochemicals, beta-carotene*, and vitamin C.

**Ingredients:**

½ cup Rose hips

2 cups Oat flour

½ tsp Baking powder

1 tsp Ground cinnamon

¼ tsp Ground cardamom

¼ cup Raisins

1/ cup Honey

1 egg Eggs + 1 yolk

2 tbsp Coconut oil

2 tspVanilla extract

**Directions:**

1. Preheat the oven to 375°F and prepare a baking sheet;
2. Cut the rose hips and remove the pits;
3. Mix together the dry ingredients;
4. Stir in rose hips and raisins;
5. In another bowl, beat the eggs, oil, honey and vanilla until smooth;
6. Incorporate the wet ingredients into the flour mixture quickly folding it;
7. Serve the cookies with an ice-cream scoop and bake for 11 to 13 minutes, until golden brown;
8. Remove them from the oven and transfer to a cooling rack.

## 37. Colorful salad

This refreshingly colorful salad is the best way to start falling in love with a green diet. Rich in flavor, this salad takes health promoting to the next level, loaded with phytochemicals, isothiocyanates, beta-carotene, and omega-3, compounds that are involved in the prevention of cancer. This salad is also a great source of vitamins and nutrients.

**Ingredients:**

2 Pink grapefruit

1 Tangerine

1 head Red Belgian endive

3cups Arugula

3 cups Baby spinach

5 cups Watercress

200 gr Smoked salmon

Half Grapefruit juice

1 Lemon juice

3 tbsp Olive oil

1 tbsp Honey

1 tsp Sriracha sauce

½ tsp Salt

Fresh Ground black pepper to taste

**Directions:**

1. Squeeze the juice of a grapefruit and a lemon and reserve for later
2. Peel and cut the grapefruit and orange, chop the arugula, watercress and spinach, cut the endives and salmon into stripes, toss everything together and add salt and pepper to taste;
3. For the vinaigrette mix the grapefruit and lemon juice, olive oil, sriracha and honey;
4. Pour the vinaigrette onto the salad, mix it until well combine;
5. Serve and enjoy!

## 38. Sweet Potato Creamy Soup

Sweet potatoes are an amazing source of beta-carotene and vitamin C, it also has unique root proteins and significant antioxidant properties, making these potatoes an excellent addition to any anti-cancer diet. In this recipe we enhance the properties by including ingredients such as: tomatoes, garlic, ginger, and chili peppers that also prevent ovarian cancer.

**Ingredients:**

2 Sweet potatoes

1 small yellow onion, diced

2 Garlic gloves, minced

2 cup Fresh tomato juice

1 Chili pepper

1 tbsp Fresh ginger

2 Vegetable broth

½ cup Walnuts

Fresh ground pepper to taste

1 tsp Salt

**Directions:**

1. In a saucepan with water cook the potatoes until soft, set aside to cool;
2. In a large saucepan sauté onions and garlic;
3. Add tomato juice, chili peppers and ginger and let it boil;
4. Meantime, peel the potatoes and put them in a food processor (or blender) and mix it along with the chicken broth, and walnuts, until it resembles to a puree;
5. Stir the potatoes mixture into the saucepan and season with salt and pepper;
6. Serve hot and enjoy.

## 39. Mustard Greens

Mustard greens have incredible health benefits and disease prevention qualities thanks to the many phyto-nutrients, vitamins, and minerals it has. It's also a rich source of flavonoids, indoles, and sulforaphane, which have been proven effective against prostate, breast, colon, and ovarian cancer treatment.

**Ingredients:**

5 cups Mustard greens

2 cups Cherry tomatoes

1 Red onion

2 Garlic gloves, minced

2 tbsp Olive oil

1 cup Chicken broth

½ tsp Salt

Fresh ground pepper to taste

1 tsp Sesame oil

1 to 2 tbsp Sesame seeds

**Directions:**

1. Wash and rinse the vegetables;
2. Chop the mustard greens, cut the onions in stripes and mince the garlic, cut the tomatoes in half and reserve;
3. Sauté the mustard greens, onions and garlic, add chicken broth and let it simmer for about 5 minutes, add sesame oil, salt and pepper to taste;
4. Incorporate the tomatoes, serve and sprinkle with sesame seeds.

## 40. Chickpeas delicacy

We know how delicious they are, but that's not their only perk. When you eat them and those beans ferment in your body, they release a metabolite called butyrate, this short-chain fatty acid is known for its efficiency on stopping the proliferation and generates *Apoptosis* (self-destruction) of cancer cells. In addition, beta-sitostirol, the central Phytosterol has shown to reduce ovarian cancer radically.

**Ingredients:**

2 cups Long rice (Basmati Rice)

2 tbsp Olive Oil

1 large onion, chopped

Kosher salt and ground pepper to taste

2 tsp Curry powder

2 Garlic gloves, chopped

1 cup vegetable stock

2 cups or 15 Oz canned chickpeas, drain and rinsed

13 Oz Coconut milk

2 tbsp Honey

2 Tbsp spicy sauce

Naan bread for serving.

**Directions:**

1. Cook Basmati Rice according to the package.

2. Heat olive oil in a medium size pan, add the onions and season them with salt and pepper; cook for 10 minutes or until onions are dark brown and caramelized.

3. Stir in the curry powder and garlic, cook for a minute.

4. Pour in the vegetable stock and scrape up all the brown bits in the pan.

5. Incorporate the chickpeas, coconut milk, honey and the spicy sauce.

6. Bring to a boil and immediately reduce heat and simmer for 10 minutes.

7. Taste and season to taste.

8. Warm up the Naan bread, serve the chickpeas and garnish with a little bit of cilantro.

## 41. Brussel-Be-Good balls

Brussel sprouts can be an incredible addition to your anti-cancer diet; not only are they low in calories, and have a very low glycemic rate, but several studies have proven that Brussels sprouts have chemo-preventive effects by altering the metabolism of carcinogens and reducing free radical damage.

**Ingredients:**

500 g Brussels sprouts

Salt and spices to taste

3 garlic gloves, dried

3 black garlic gloves

Olive oil Extra-Virgin

Black pepper to taste

**Directions:**

1. In a pan sauté garlic with olive oil.

2. When the garlic gets a bit golden, add the Brussels sprouts, cover it with a lid and let it simmer for 6-7 minutes.

3. Remove the lid and incorporate salt with spices, black pepper, and black garlic coat it with olive oil cover it again with a lid and let it simmer so it cooks in its own juice and the Brussels sprouts get aromatized of the garlic and spices.

4. Be careful not to dry the mixture. And stir occasionally.

5. When the Brussels sprouts can be cut easily stop cooking and serve them.

## 42. Scallion's omelet

Scallions are very well known because of their healing properties, highlighting the digestive enhancing properties. This *Alliums Vegetable* helps to maintain the intestinal flora that benefits the elimination of dangerous toxins and is also rich in vitamin B, C, and minerals which are very important to keep our antioxidant system working and eliminating free radicals that create cancer.

**Ingredients:**

As much scallions you want to use

3 eggs, beaten

1 garlic glove *optional

Salt to taste

Olive oil

**Directions:**

1. Wash and rinse the scallions

2. Sauté in a pan the scallions with olive oil and garlic if using it; cook until scallions change their color to a dark green.

3. Incorporate the eggs and stir a bit. And let it cook

4. When the base in hardened and the surface if a bit hardened too, turn it around.

5. Let it cook for 2 minutes and serve.

## ADDITIONAL TITLES FROM THIS AUTHOR

70 Effective Meal Recipes to Prevent and Solve Being Overweight: Burn Fat Fast by Using Proper Dieting and Smart Nutrition

By

Joe Correa CSN


48 Acne Solving Meal Recipes: The Fast and Natural Path to Fixing Your Acne Problems in Less Than 10 Days!

By

Joe Correa CSN


41 Alzheimer's Preventing Meal Recipes: Reduce or Eliminate Your Alzheimer's Condition in 30 Days or Less!

By

Joe Correa CSN


70 Effective Breast Cancer Meal Recipes: Prevent and Fight Breast Cancer with Smart Nutrition and Powerful Foods

By

Joe Correa CSN

www.ingramcontent.com/pod-product-compliance
Lightning Source LLC
Chambersburg PA
CBHW070156080526
44586CB00015B/2012